TIME
FOR KIDS

Staying
Healthy

D0104228

Dona Herweck Rice

Consultant

Timothy Rasinski, Ph.D.
Kent State University

Publishing Credits

Dona Herweck Rice, *Editor-in-Chief*
Lee Aucoin, *Creative Director*
Conni Medina, M.A.Ed., *Editorial Director*
Jamey Acosta, *Editor*
Robin Erickson, *Designer*
Stephanie Reid, *Photo Editor*
Rachelle Cracchiolo, M.S.Ed., *Publisher*

Image Credits

Cover Photolibrary; p.4 visionaryft/Shutterstock; p.5 Monkey Business Images/Shutterstock; p.6 Andresr/Shutterstock; p.7 wavebreakmedia ltd/Shutterstock; p.8 Stuart Monk/Shutterstock; p.9 Forster Forest/Shutterstock; p.10 kali9/iStockphoto; p.11 Monkey Business Images/iStockphoto; p.12 AlexRaths/iStockphoto; p.13 sjlocke/iStockphoto; p.14 matka_Wariatka/Shutterstock; p.15 tan4ikk/Shutterstock; p.16 ranplett/iStockphoto; p.17 Rich Legg/iStockphoto; p.18 3445128471/Shutterstock; p.19 Studio 1One/Shutterstock; back cover Garsya/Shutterstock

Based on writing from *TIME For Kids*

TIME For Kids and the *TIME For Kids* logo are registered trademarks of TIME Inc. Used under license.

Teacher Created Materials

5301 Oceanus Drive
Huntington Beach, CA 92649-1030
http://www.tcmpub.com
ISBN 978-1-4333-3595-2

Copyright © 2012 by Teacher Created Materials, Inc.

BP 5028

Table of Contents

Staying Healthy 4

Eating Right 6

Drinking Water 8

Running and Playing . 10

Seeing the Doctor . . . 12

Sleeping 14

Using Your Mind 16

Words to Know 20

Staying Healthy

You are growing fast now. You need to take good care of yourself.

This book will tell you
what to do to stay healthy.

Eating Right

The right foods help you grow strong. Fruit and vegetables are good.

Make healthy choices. Eat snacks but not too many.

"How about some chips, Mom?" you ask.

She says, "Okay, but no cookies this time."

Drinking Water

Did you know your body needs lots of water? It is better for you than juice and soda. Water helps to keep you healthy.

Water also helps to keep you clean. Being clean is part of being healthy.

Running and Playing

Run every day. It makes you strong. Playing sports is a good way to run and have some fun.

Play every day, too.
Playing makes you happy.
Being happy is good for
you.

Seeing the Doctor

See the doctor for checkups. The nurse will weigh and measure you to see how much you have grown.

"My, you are growing!"
she will say.

"Yes, you are right," you
can tell her.

Sleeping

Get a good sleep every night. Being tired is no fun.

When you sleep well, you will be ready for the next day. You will feel good.

Using Your Mind

Your mind needs to be strong, too. You use your mind every day, no matter what you do.

Are you using your mind right now? Yes, you are. Good for you!

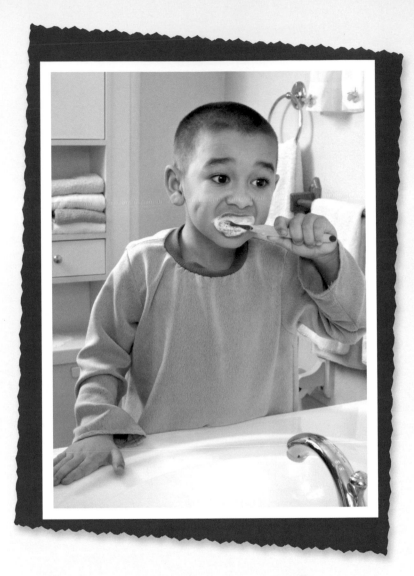

Take good care of
yourself.

You will be glad you did.

Words to Know

body	nurse
care	playing
check-ups	right
choices	running
doctor	sleeping
drinking	sports
eating	staying
fruit	strong
growing	tired
grown	vegetables
healthy	water
measure	weigh
minds	yourself